REPTILES!

Coloring Book

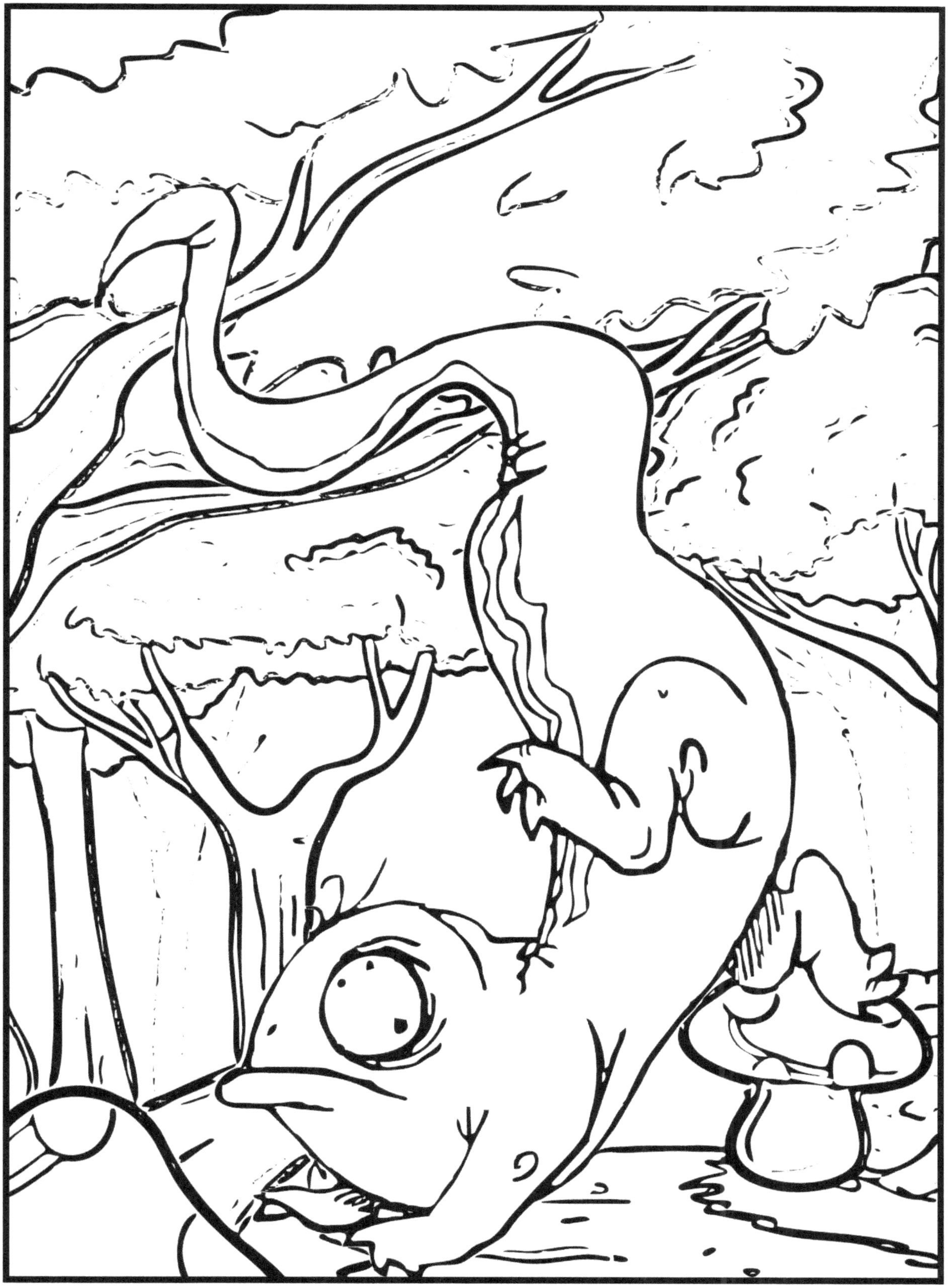

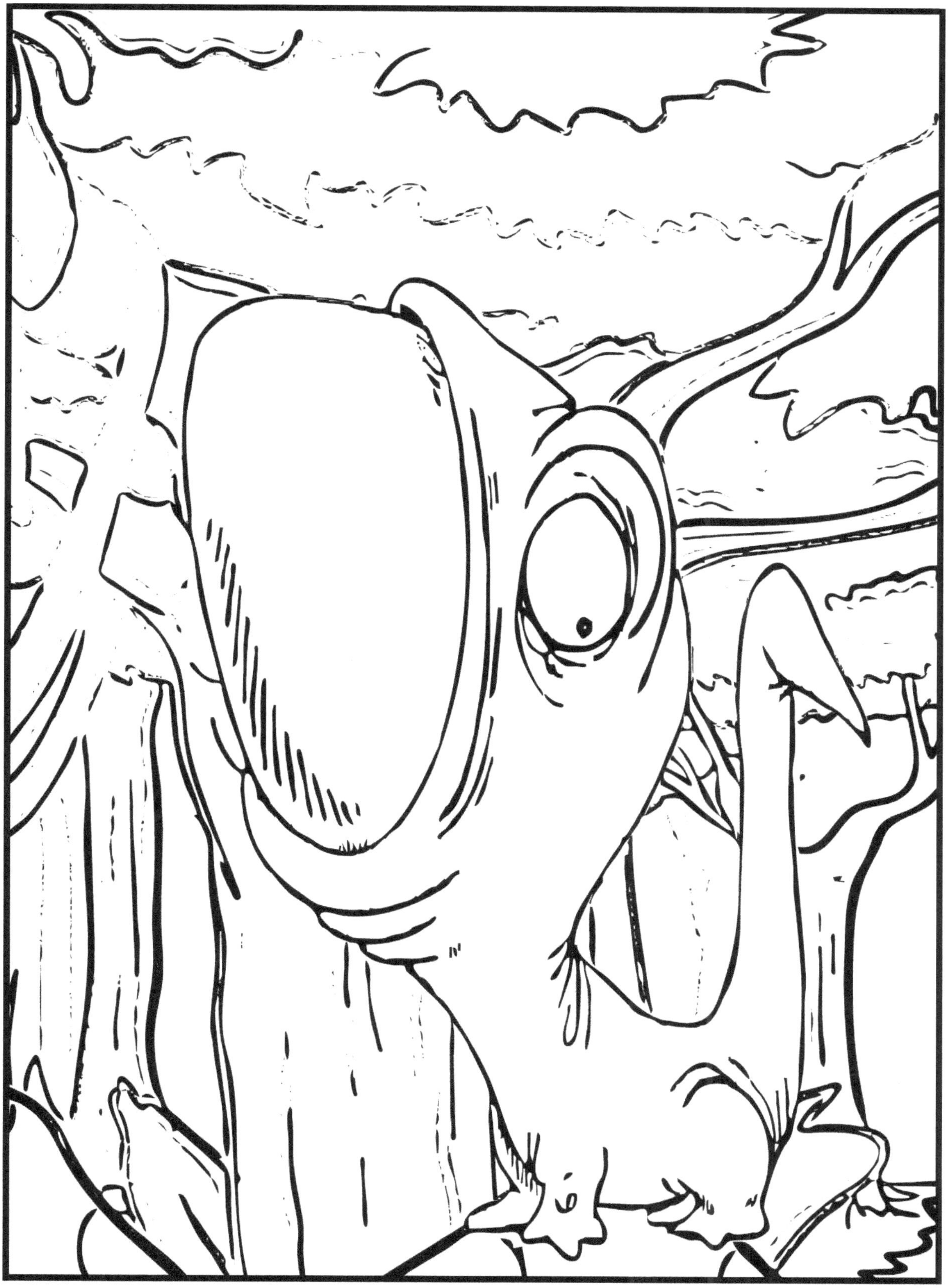

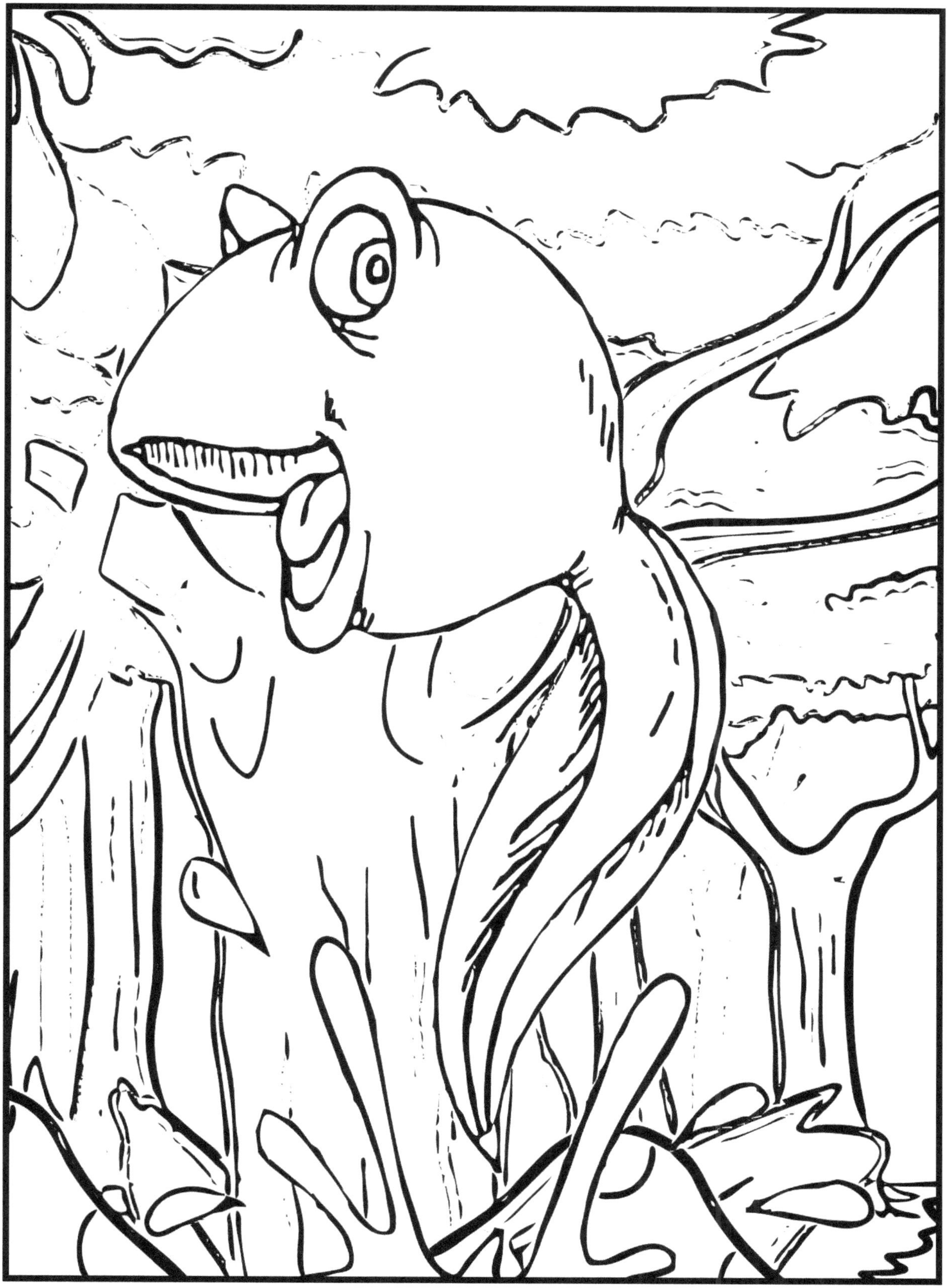

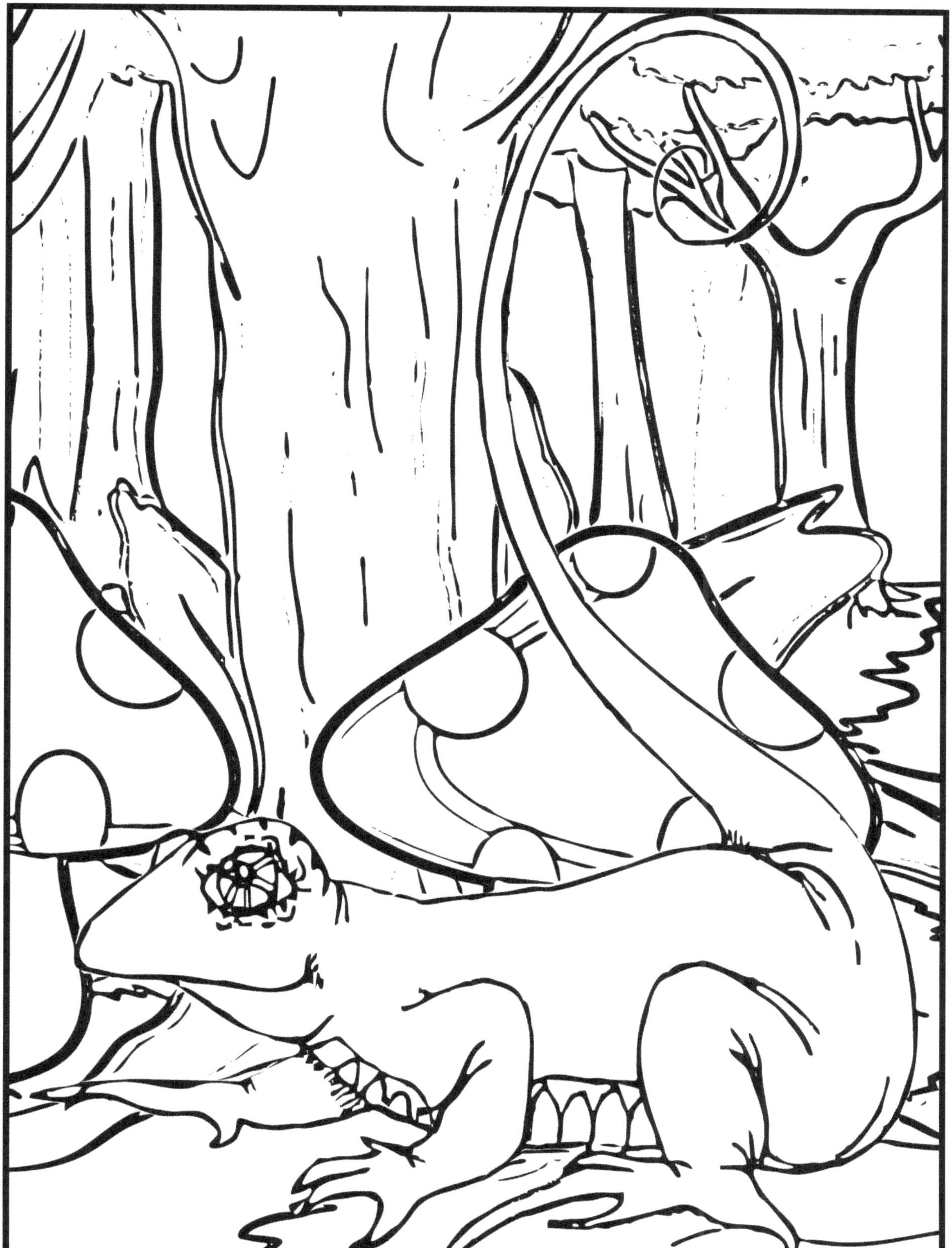

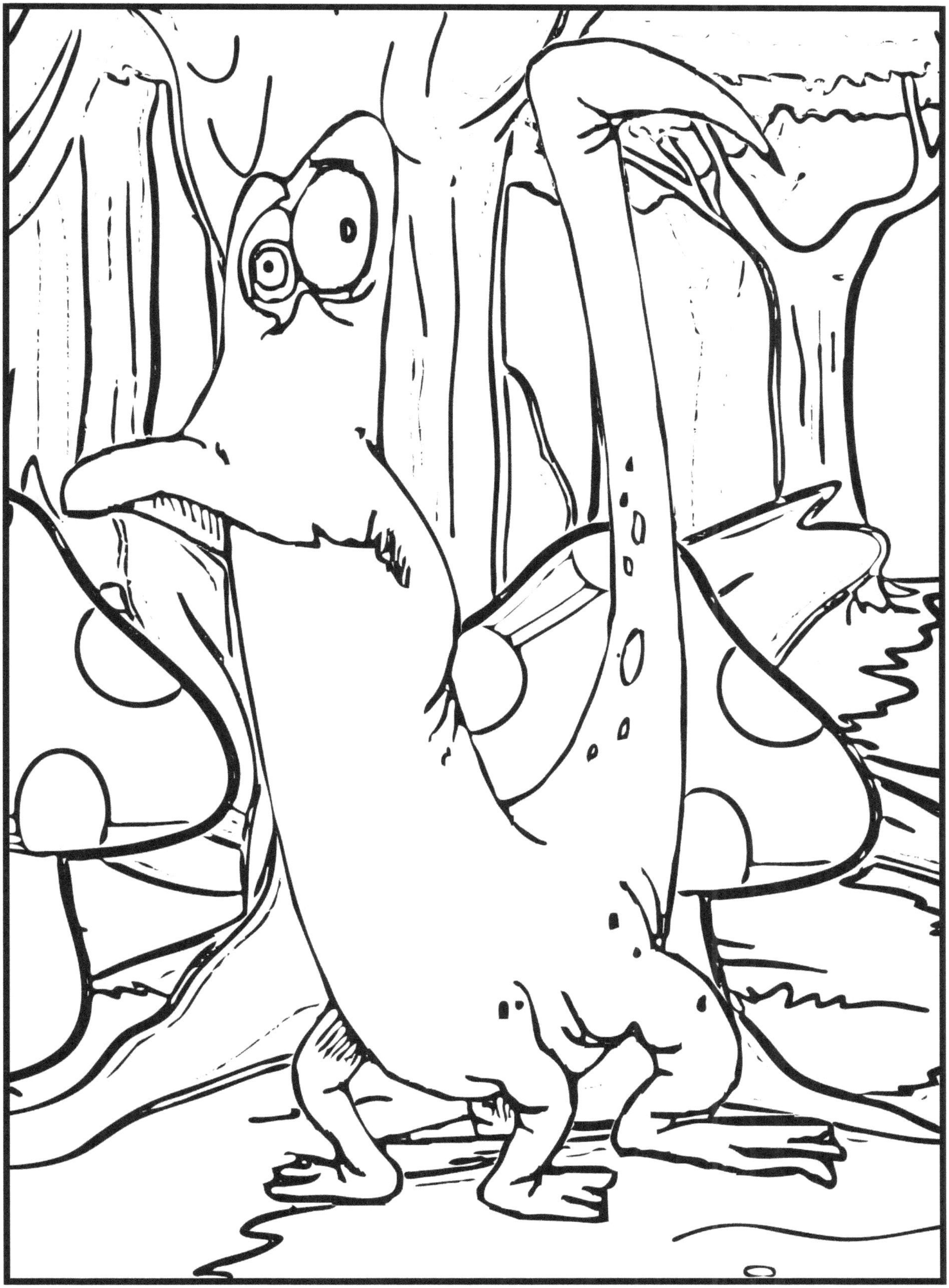

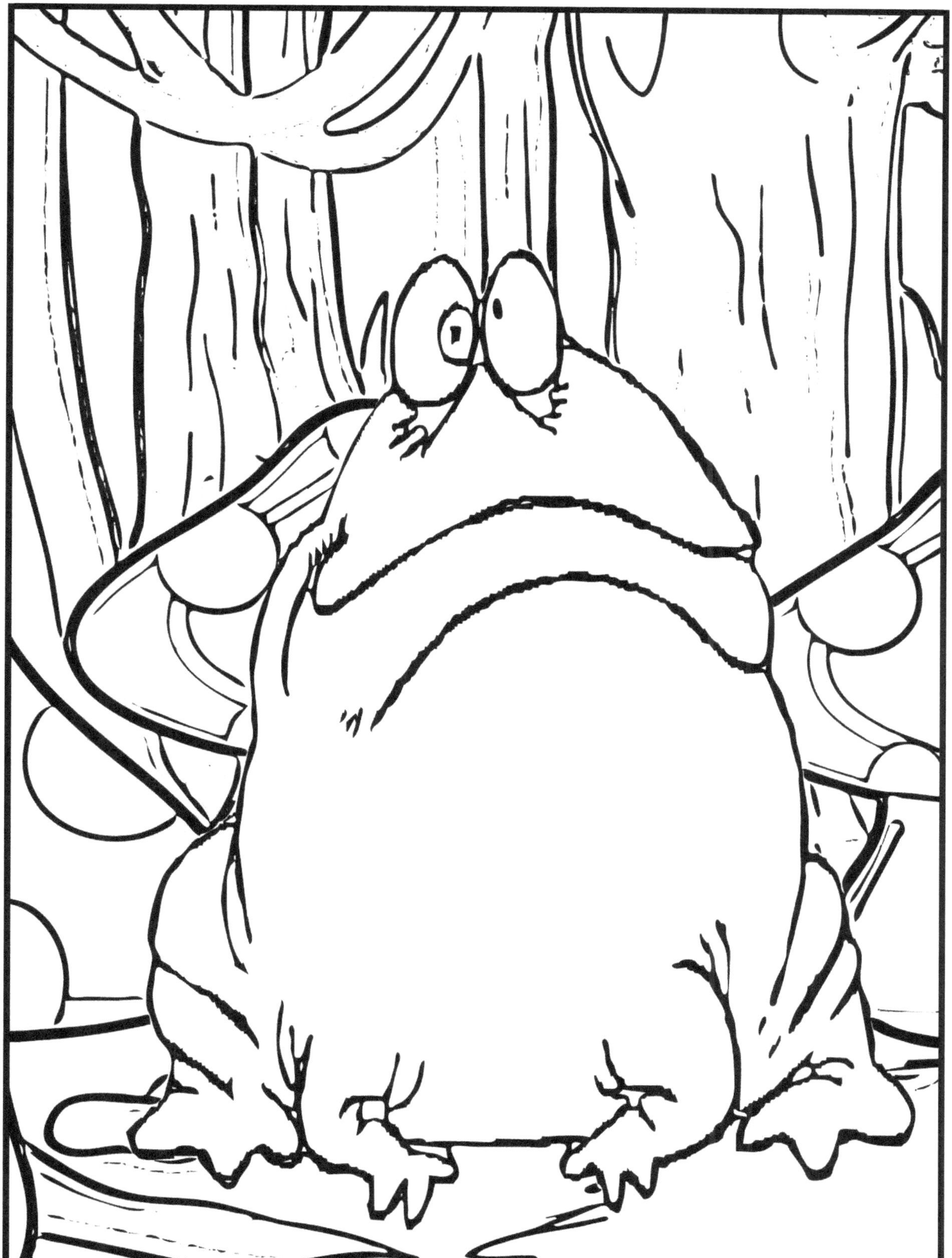

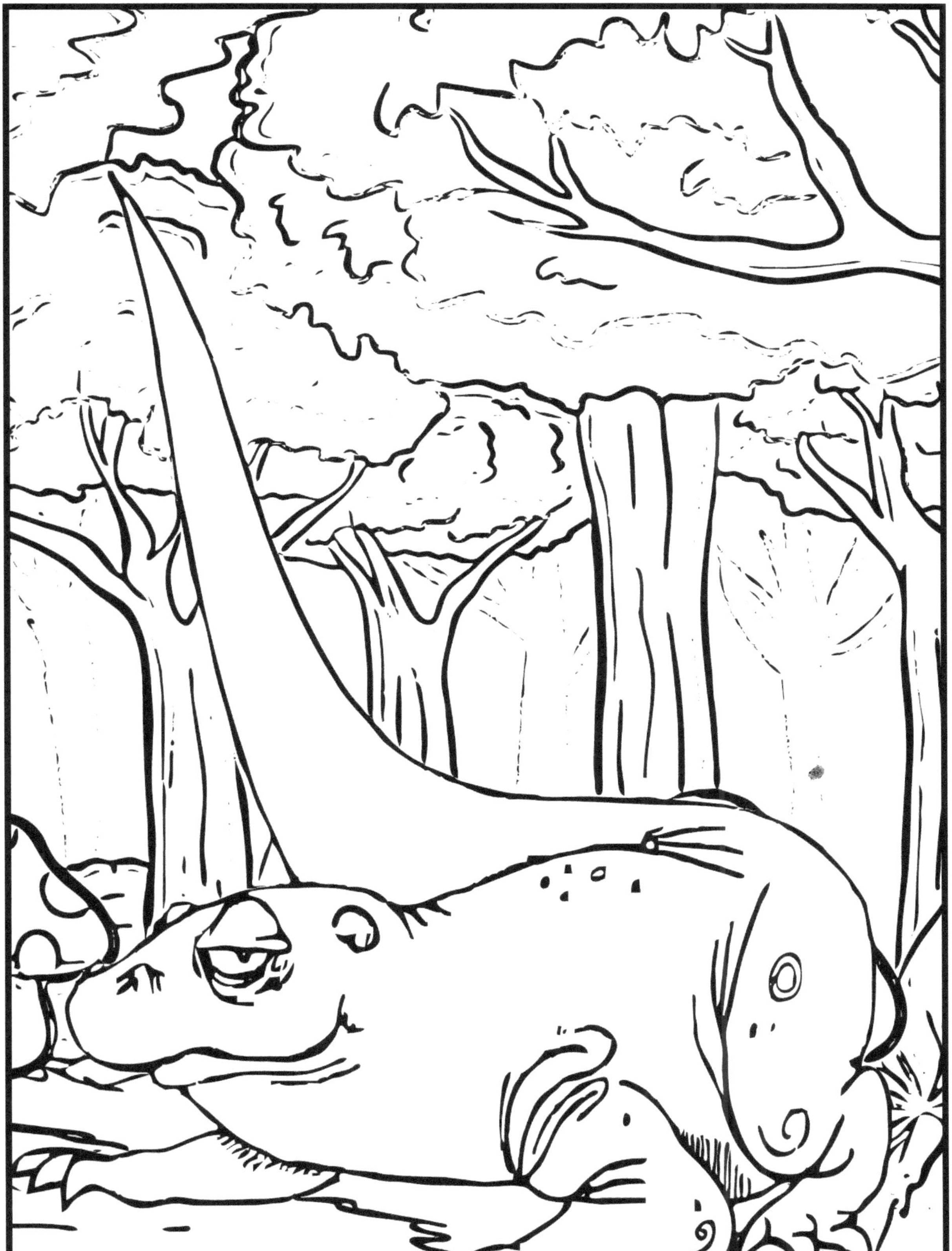

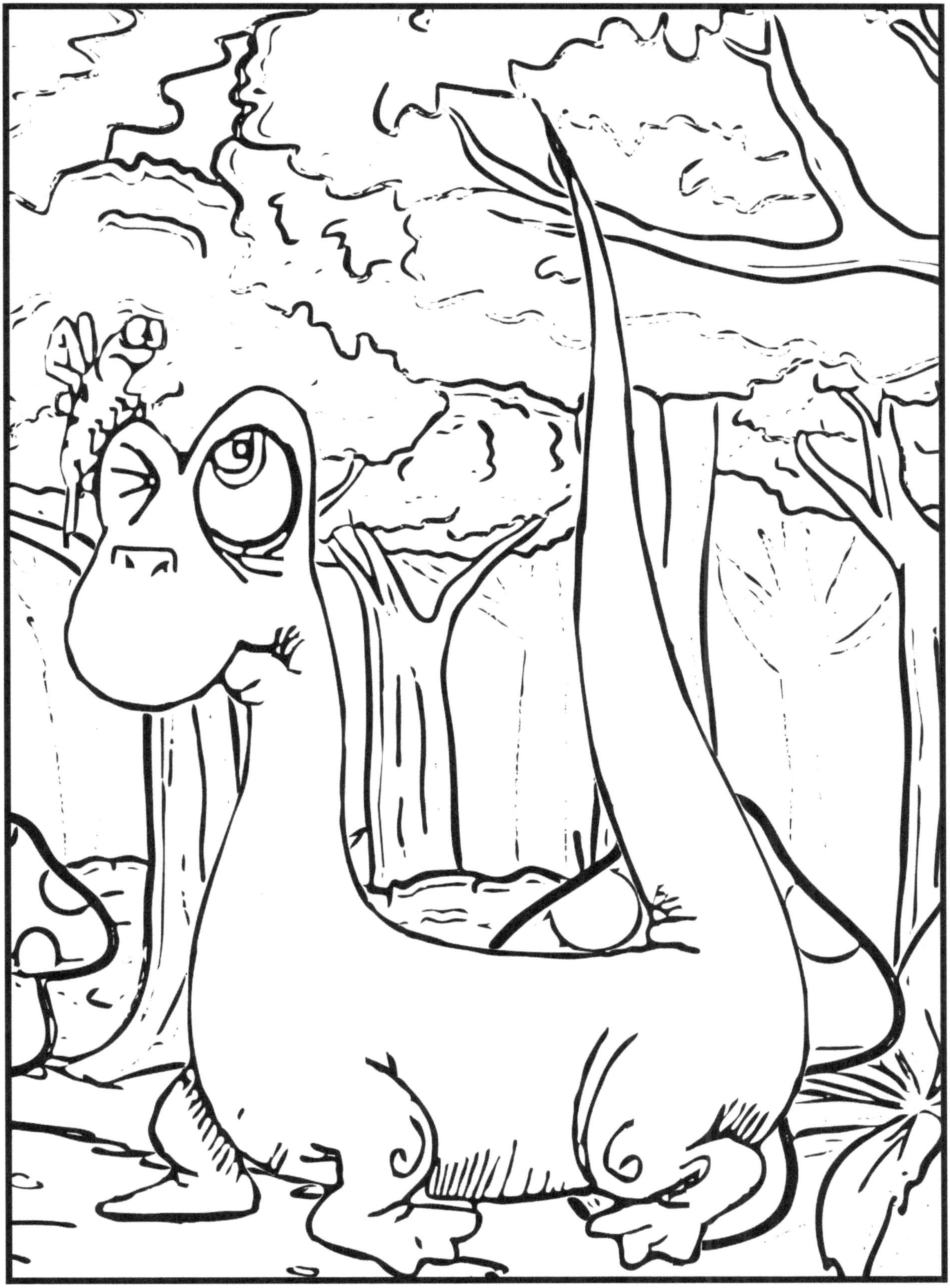

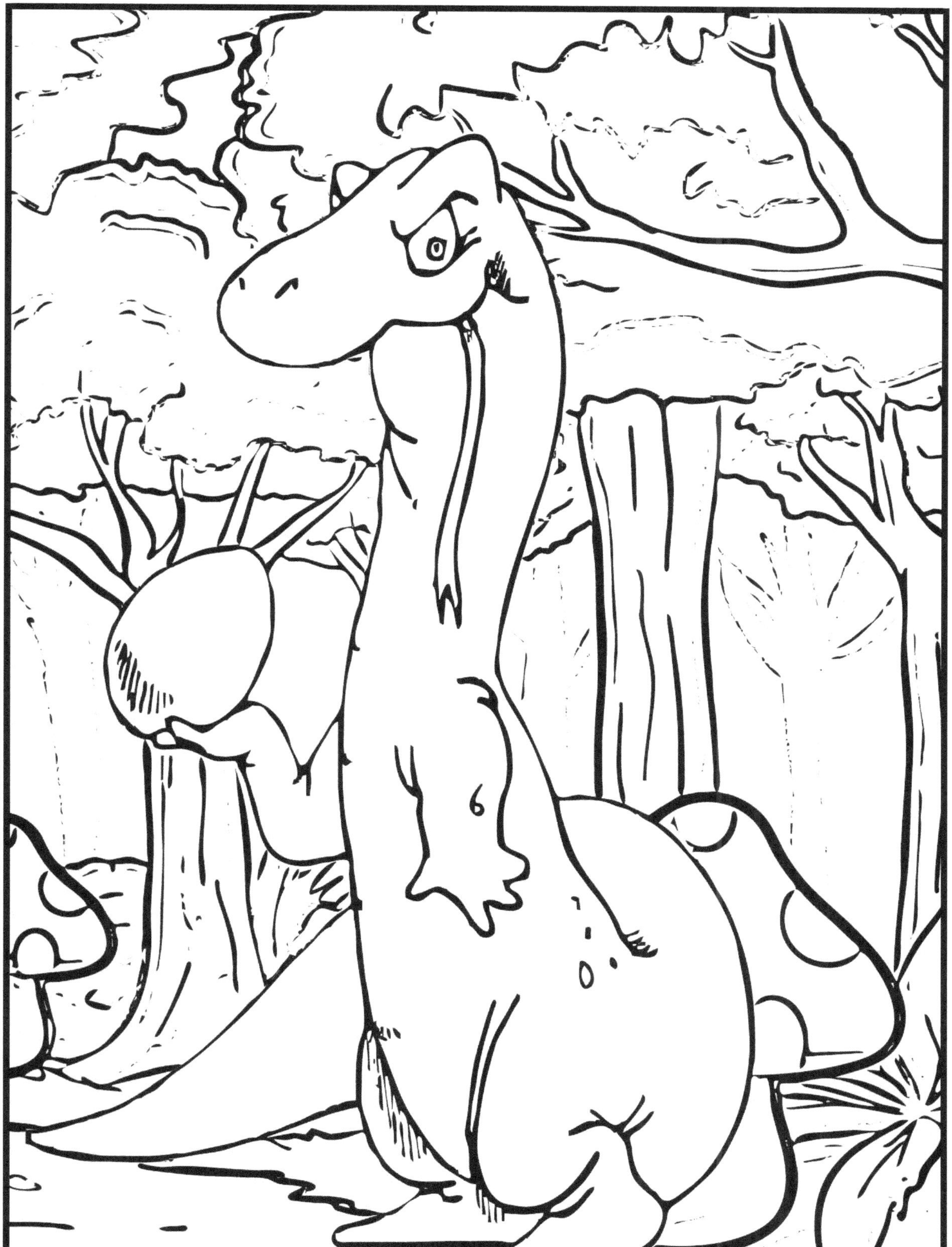

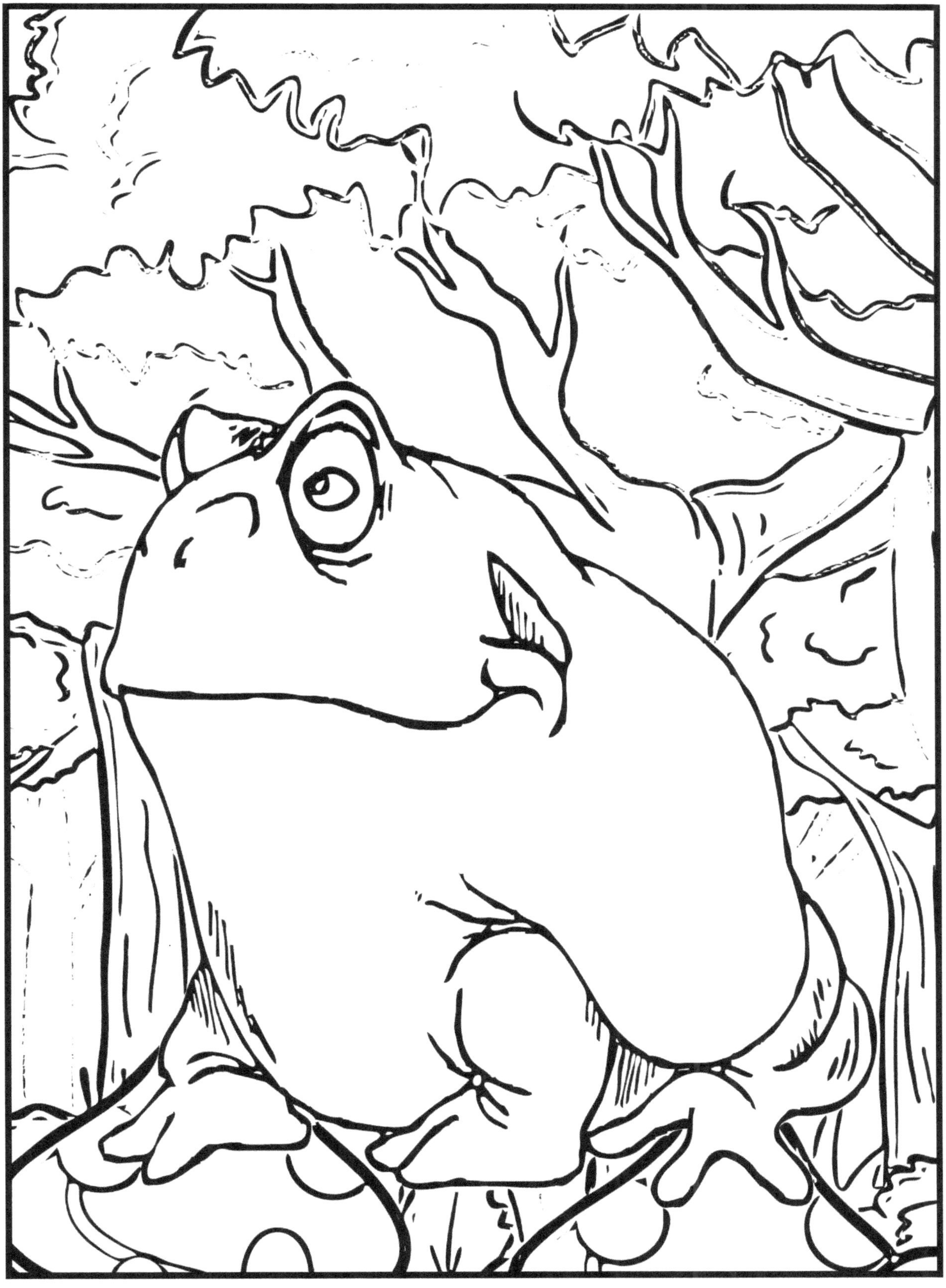

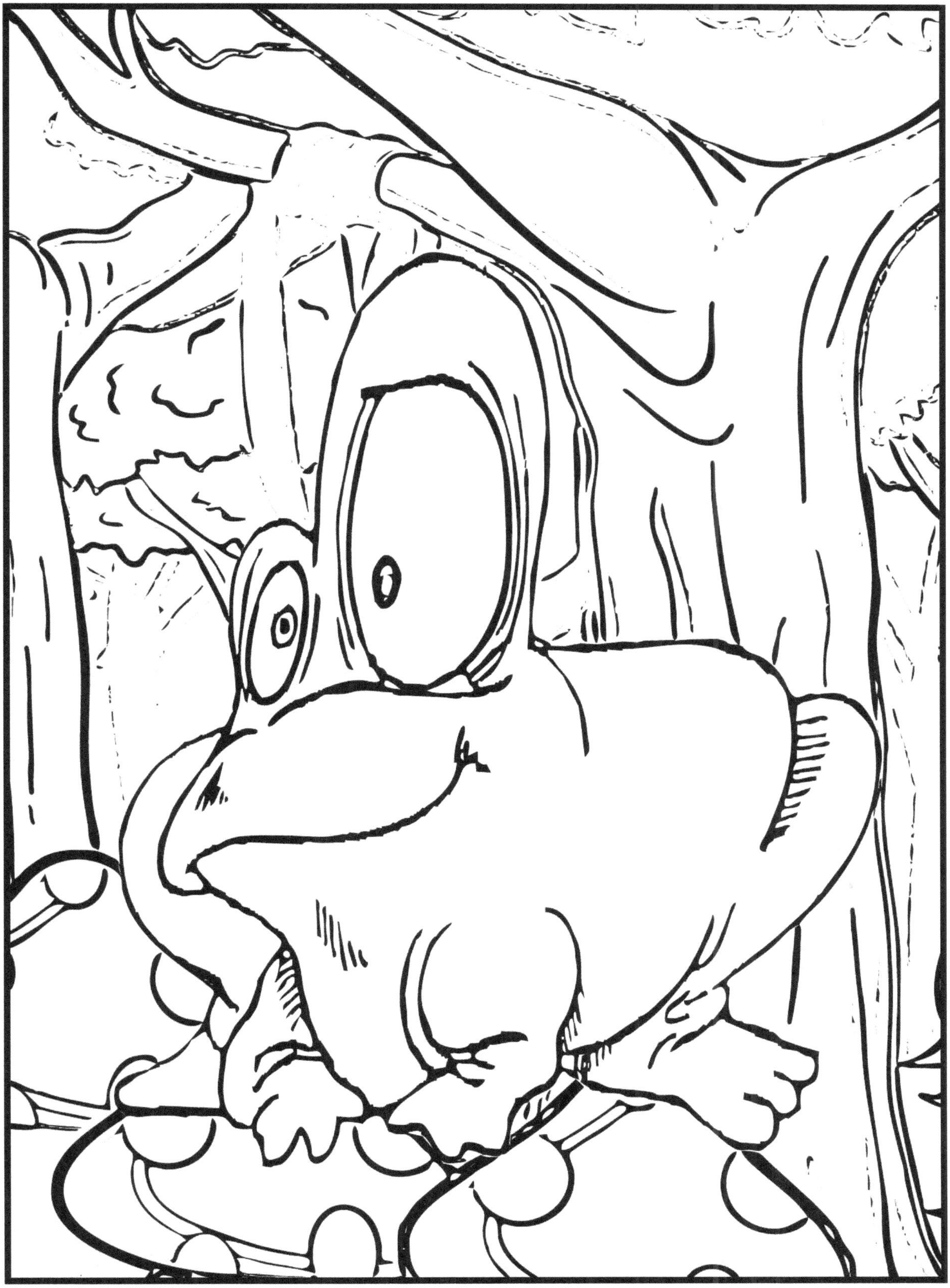

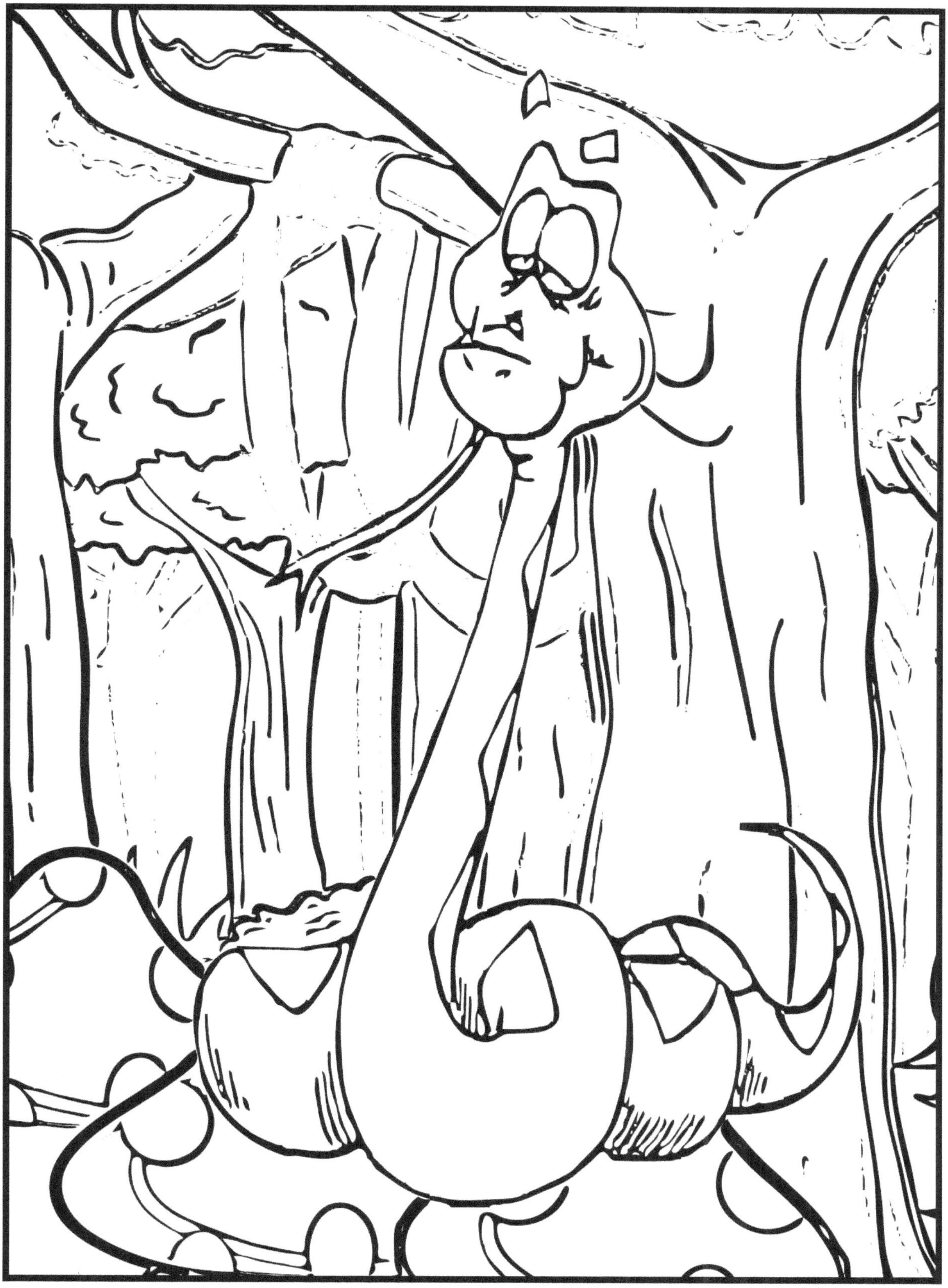

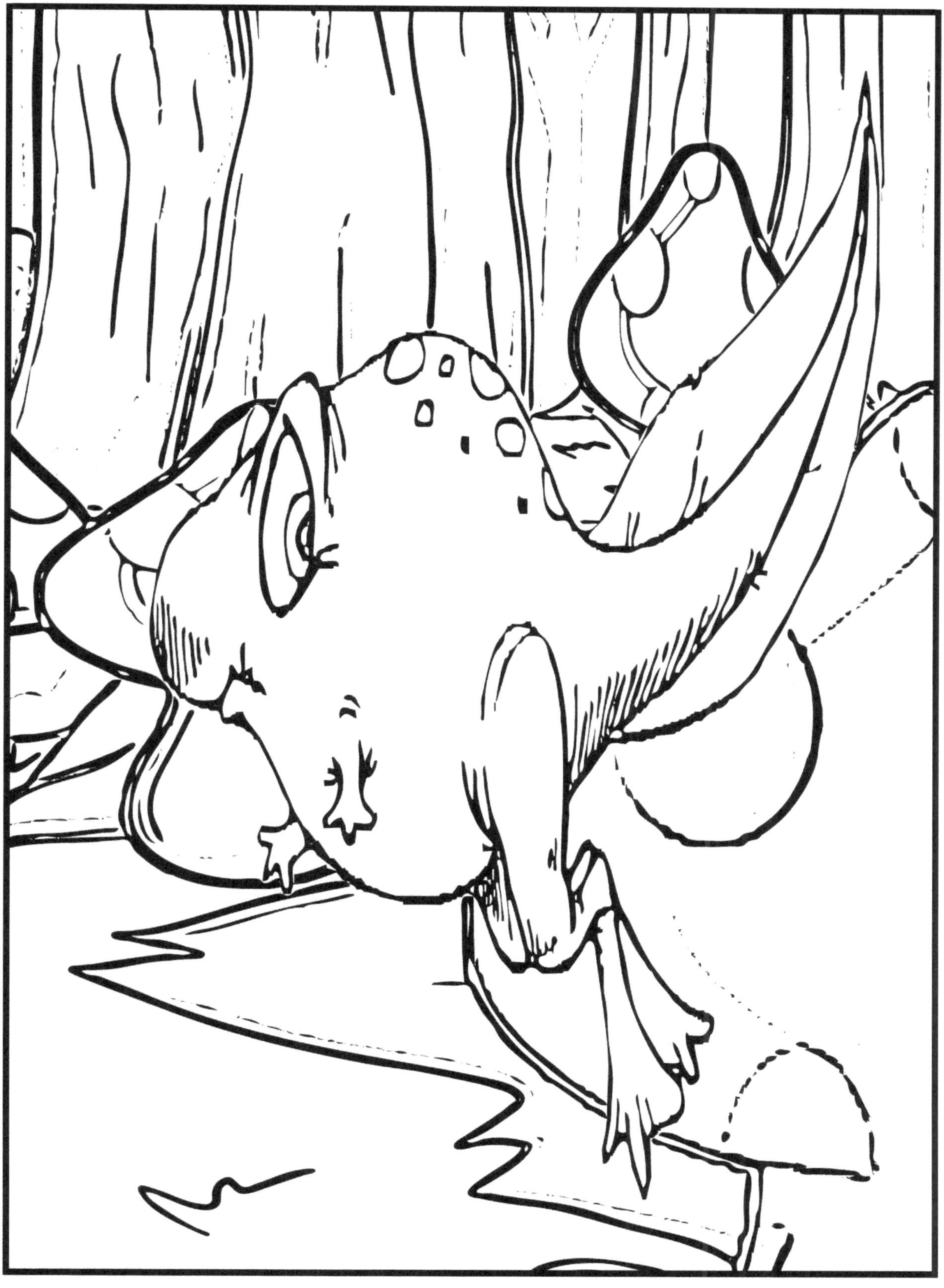

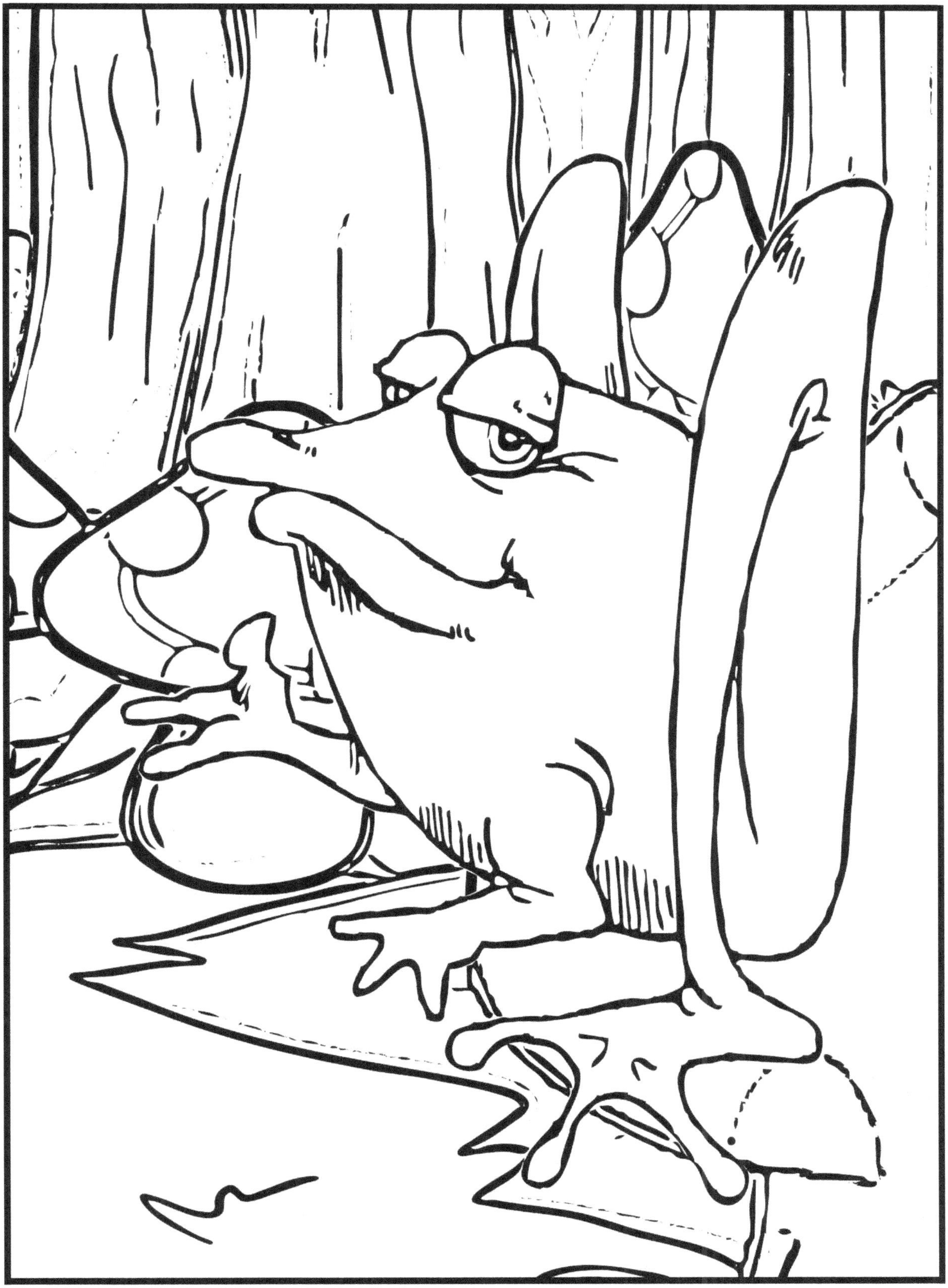

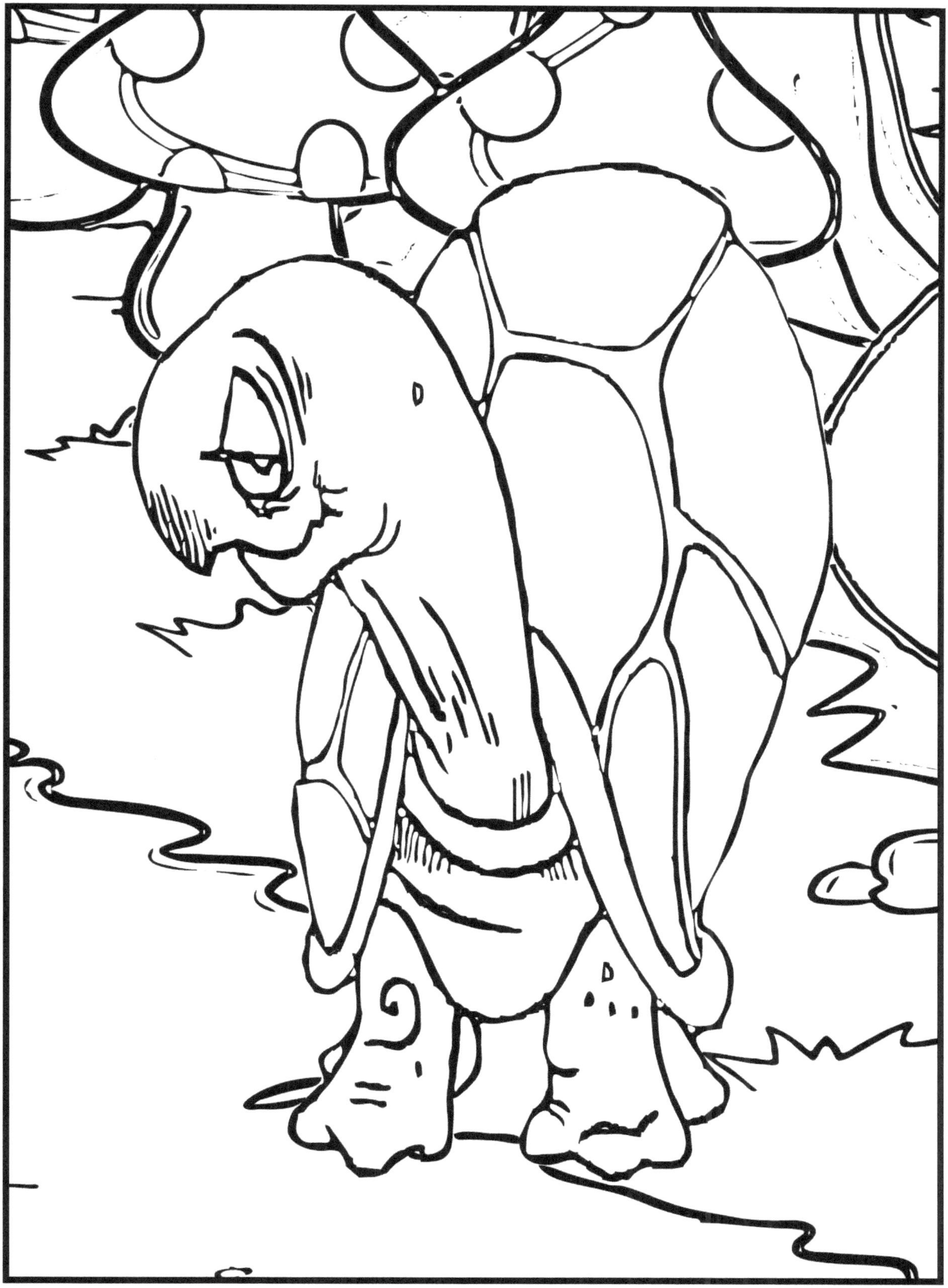

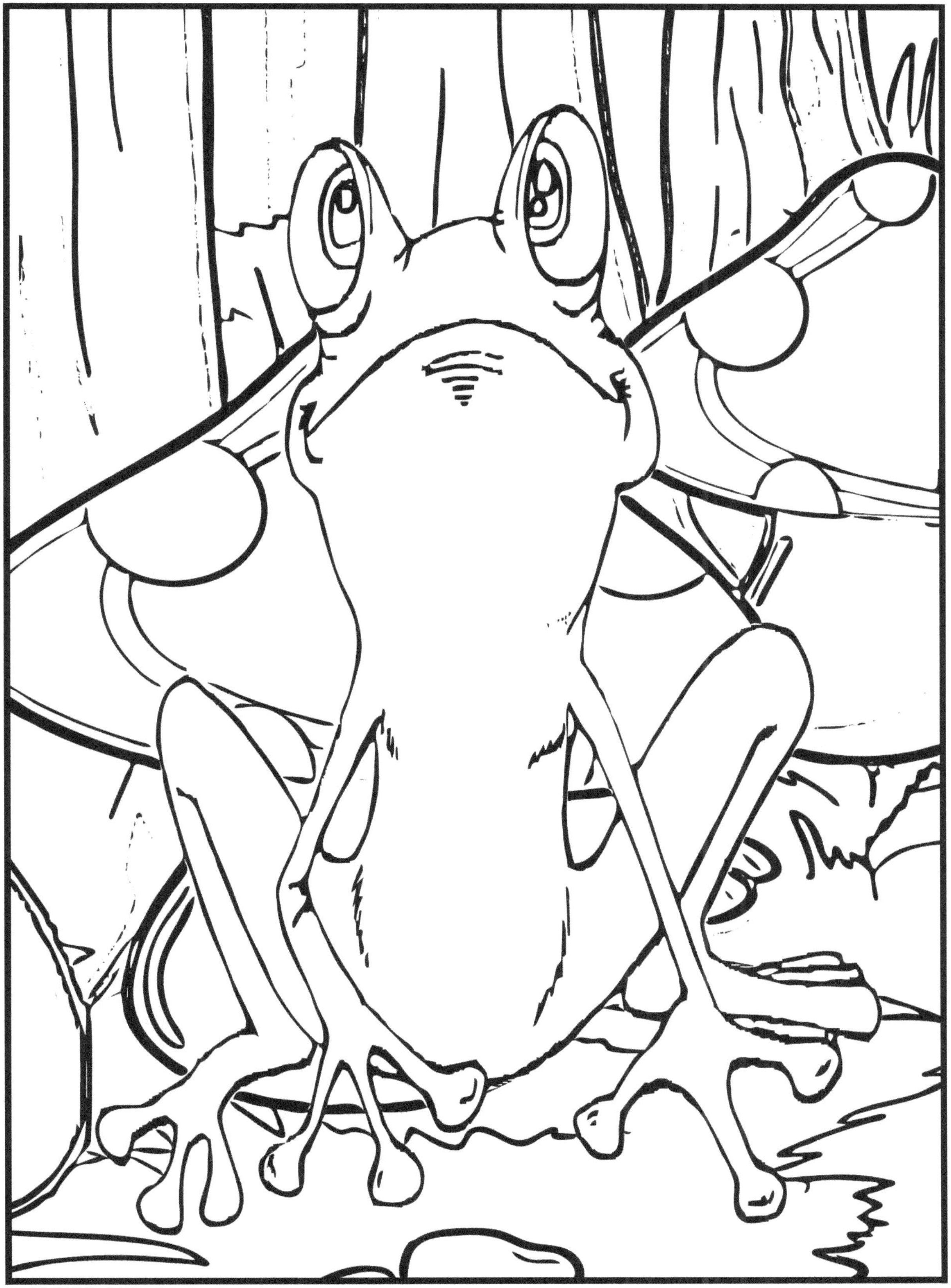

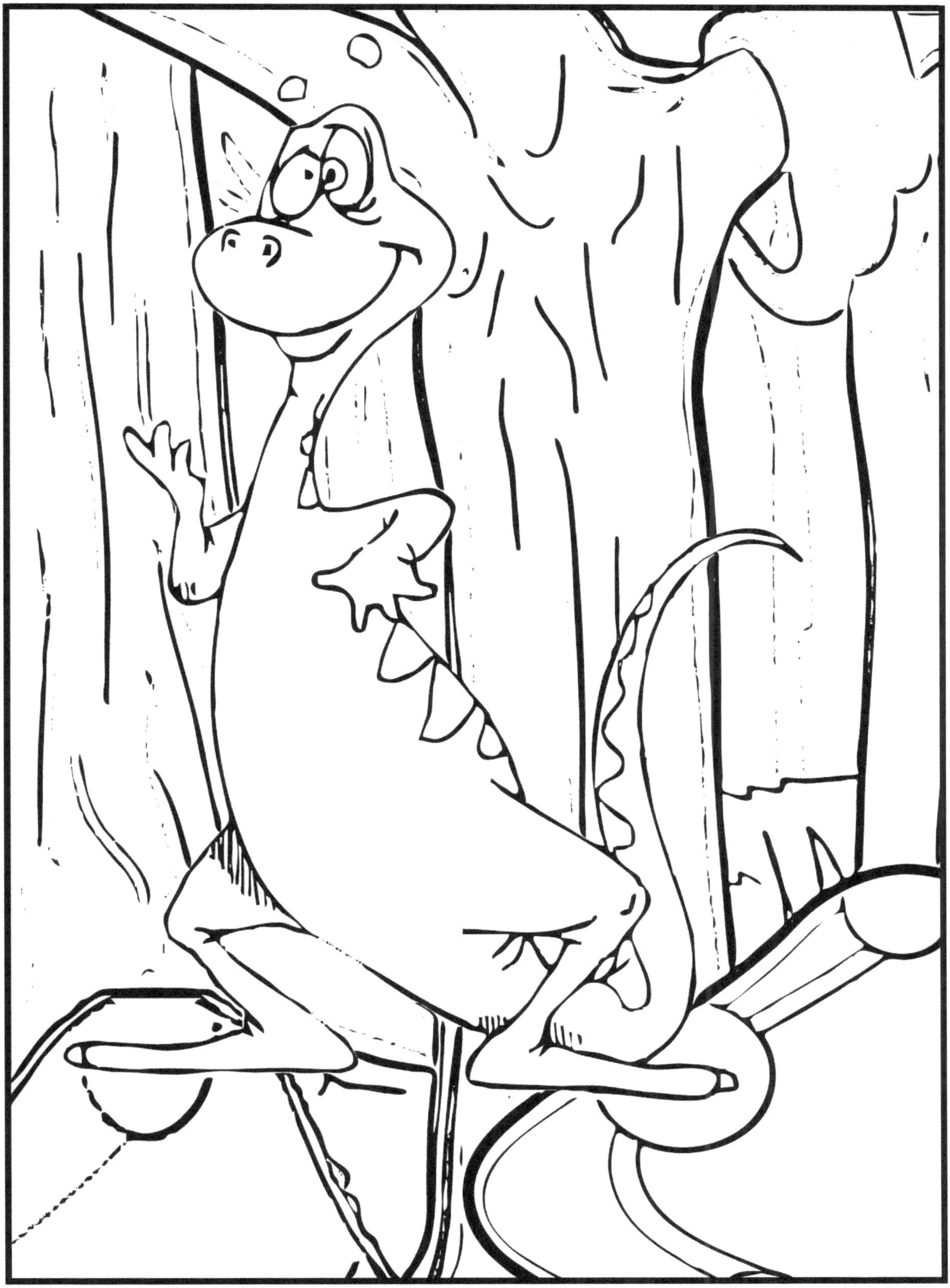

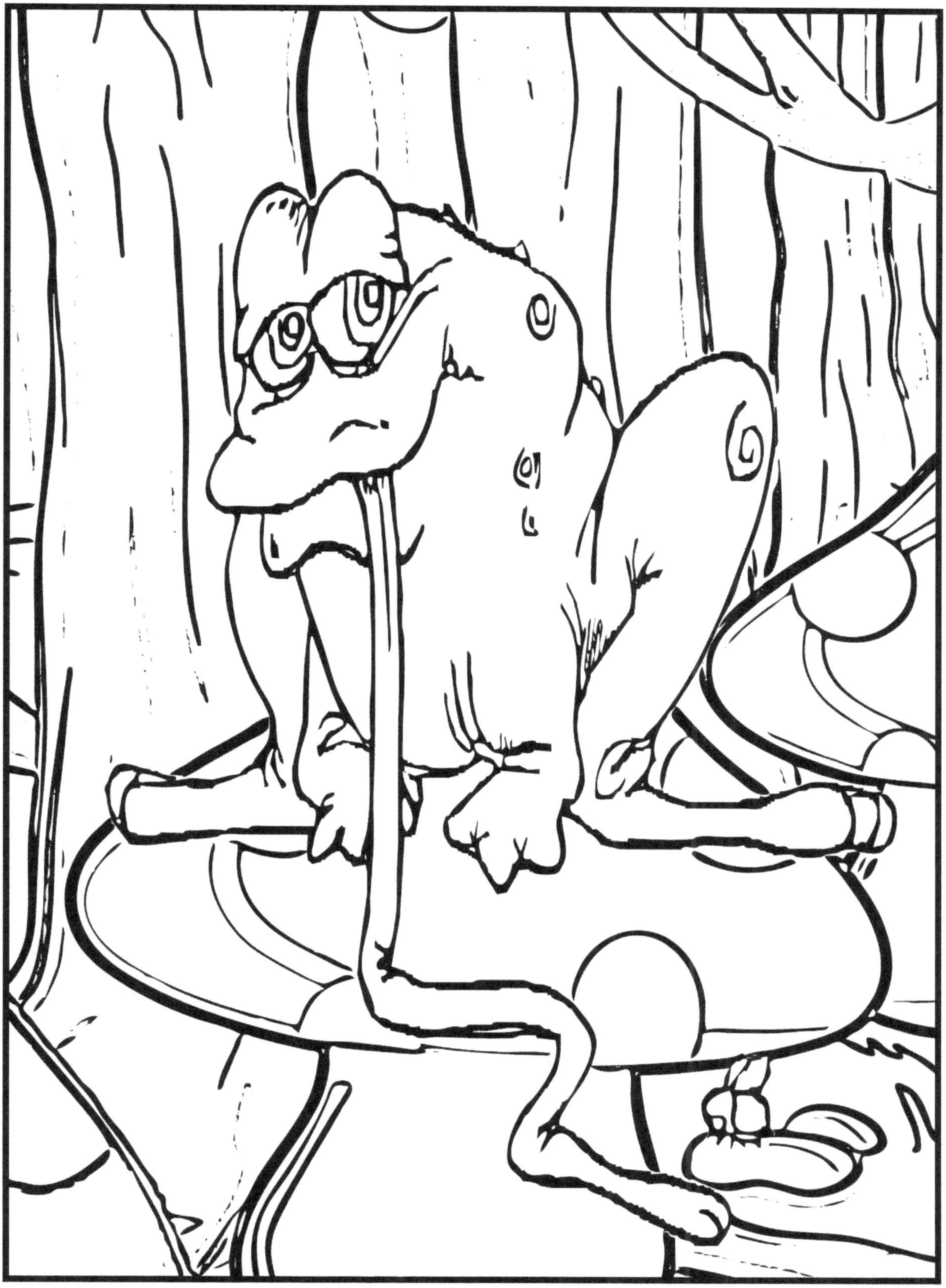

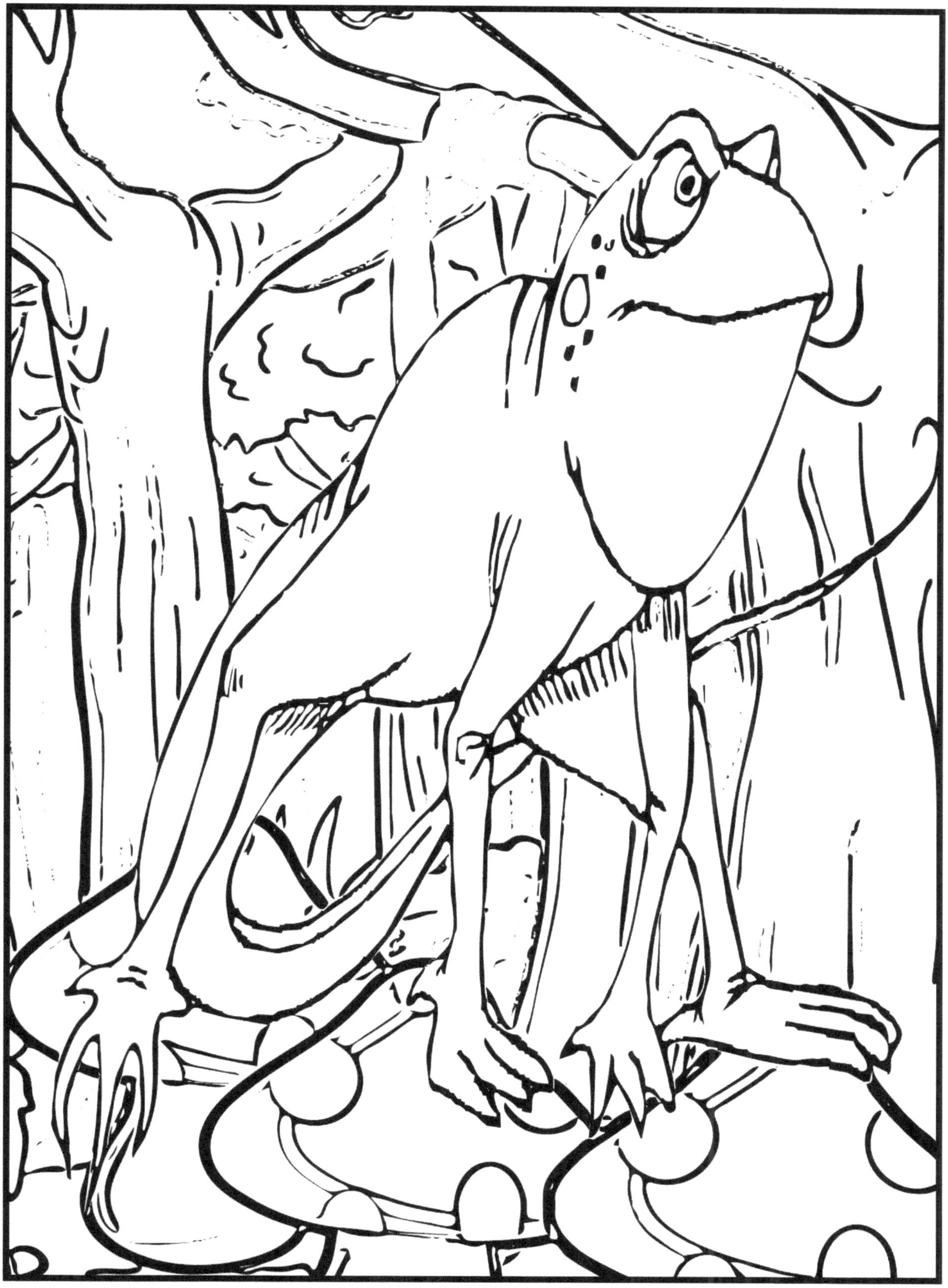

www.ingramcontent.com/pod-product-compliance
Lightning Source LLC
Chambersburg PA
CBHW081404170526
45166CB00010B/3204
* 9 7 8 1 5 1 9 7 7 5 5 6 6 *